SCHUMANN

In memory of
Stella (Stelle)
Stephanie Czopor,
mother of Carol Brackeen and
Ed Czopor Jr.
This book is a tribute to her
special love of reading, sincere
involvement and genuine respect
for young children.
Donated to
the Children's Workshop

Collection by Manny, Jean, & Emma Lucero

Date 2003

For Trevor and Daniel remembering
"the little antelope" where it all began!

First edition for the United States, Canada,
and the Philippines published 1993
by Barron's Educational Series, Inc.

Design David West Children's Book Design

© Copyright by Aladdin Books Ltd 1993
Copyright in the text © Ann Rachlin / Fun with Music

Designed and produced by
Aladdin Books Ltd
28 Percy Street
London W1P 9FF

All inquiries should be addressed to:
Barron's Educational Series, Inc.
250 Wireless Boulevard
Hauppauge, NY 11788

International Standard Book No. 0-8120-1544-4

Library of Congress Catalog Card No. 92-26965

Library of Congress Cataloging-in-Publication Data
Rachlin, Ann.
    Schumann / by Ann Rachlin ; illustrated by Susan Hellard.
    p. cm. – (Famous Children)
    Summary : A biography of the nineteenth-century German composer
with emphasis on his childhood and early musical training.
ISBN 0-8120-1544-4
1. Schumann, Robert, 1810-1856–Childhood and youth–Juvenile
literature. 2. Composers–Germany–Biography–Juvenile literature.
[1. Schumann, Robert, 1810-1856–Childhood and youth.
 2. Composers.] I. Hellard,Susan. ill. II.Title. III. Series:
Rachlin, Ann. Famous children.
ML3930.S39R3 1993
780'.92–dc20
[B]   92-26965
                                   CIP
                                 AC MN

Printed in Belgium
3456 98765432

Famous Children

SCHUMANN

Ann Rachlin
ILLUSTRATED BY Susan Hellard

BARRON'S

The streets of Zwickau were filled with excited people. It was 1812 and the French army was marching through the little German town on its way to Russia. The sound of drums and marching feet filled the streets and the crowd began to cheer. Sitting on his father's shoulders, little Robert Schumann had a perfect view.

"I can see the Emperor's carriage, Father!" he cried. The Emperor Napoleon and his Empress smiled and waved to the crowds as their carriage rumbled by, followed by a band of musicians. Robert clapped his hands in time to the music.

When Robert went to bed that night, the sound of the band was still ringing in his ears. The next day, Robert pretended he was the Emperor Napoleon.

"I need a coat, Ziff," he said to his kitten. Quickly pulling down his father's best coat, Robert put it on. It dragged on the floor but Robert didn't care.

Left! Right! Left! Right! Robert marched down the street to his friends.

"Attention!" he called. The boys laughed at the tiny figure in the long coat dragging in the mud.

"I'm the Emperor Napoleon," he called. "Get into line. Hurry up. Left! Right! Left! Right!" Soon the boys were marching up and down to Robert's commands.

Later, as Robert was marching home by himself, he saw a group of travelers arrive at the inn.

"They would make a good army," thought Robert and he ran over to them, shouting, "Attention! Get in line there. Quick, march." The travelers smiled but took no notice of the small Napoleon. Robert lost his temper. He marched over and hit one of the men with his stick. At that moment his father came around the corner.

Robert's father was furious. Everyone in Zwickau knew August Schumann's bookstore in the main square. Robert's rude behavior brought disgrace on the whole family. His father marched him home and sent him to sit in the punishment corner for several hours.

The youngest of five children, Robert Schumann was very bright. He spent every spare moment in his father's shop, reading. He liked poetry best and every evening he would recite the long poems he had read with his father. He loved the music of the rhyming verses and never forgot a single line.

It was the middle of the night. The house was quiet but inside Robert's head the sound of music kept him awake. He tiptoed downstairs to the piano. He sat down and tried to pick out the notes of the music in his head. He couldn't find them. Tears began to trickle down his cheeks as he realized he did not know how to play his own music.

Mrs. Schumann woke her husband.

"Someone's crying," she said. Edward, Carl and Julius were sleeping peacefully. So was Emilie. But Robert's bed was empty. They hurried downstairs. There was Robert, tears streaming down his face.

"The music, Mama. I can't find the music."

Gently they took him back to bed and tucked him in, saying,

"You can try again tomorrow, Robert. Now you must go to sleep."

"Perhaps Robert should have music lessons," said Mr. Schumann. Mrs. Schumann was doubtful.

"He might want to become a musician and then he would always be poor and hungry."

"He must do what makes him happy," said Mr. Schumann. "I'll talk to Johann Kuntsch tomorrow."

So Mr. Kuntsch the organist began teaching Robert to write music down as well as play it on the piano.

Robert was happy. Whistling down the street with Ziff nestled inside his jacket, he saw his friends.

"We're going to sail our boats. Do you want to come?" they asked.

"I'll get my yacht," cried Robert.

The fleet of toy boats struggled in the fast flowing current.

"An army has a general. A navy needs an admiral," announced Robert. "Admiral Ziff will take command," he declared and put his terrified cat on the deck of his tiny yacht. The boys cheered.

The happy cries of the boys turned to groans of horror as the strong current carried the little boat away so quickly that it was soon out of sight. Robert and the boys searched and searched. They found the boat, but the cat was nowhere to be seen. Robert went home in tears.

Every morning Robert thought he could feel Ziff's warm body at the foot of his bed. But when he opened his eyes, they filled with tears. Ziff was still missing. One night while Robert slept, a tiny, bedraggled, scruffy, black cat climbed in through Robert's window. When Robert woke up he thought he heard purring. He stretched out his hand and felt the warm fur. Ziff was back.

One evening, Robert and his mother went to a concert in Carlsbad. Robert was very excited. As the famous pianist Moscheles gave his recital, Robert clutched his program tightly in his hand. He was spellbound. One day he would play the piano like Moscheles.

"I'll never forget this night," he whispered to his mother. "And I'll keep my program forever," he murmured. And he did.

Not long afterward, Robert and Mr. Kuntsch were waiting to go on stage. The audience was seated and the singers were on the platform. Robert's mouth was dry. His first public concert! No wonder he was nervous. Robert walked to the piano. Mr. Kuntsch gave the signal and Robert began to play. The music was very difficult but he played it perfectly.

The next day everyone was talking about little Robert Schumann. The people of Zwickau were so proud of him that they invited him to give a concert all by himself.

"I won't play on that terrible piano again," he told Mr. Kuntsch. "I must have a good piano if I am to play in public. Mr. Schiffner has a wonderful piano. I'll borrow his."

"What makes you think you can borrow my piano?" Mr. Schiffner was astounded.

"I play well, sir," replied Robert, "but that piano at the hall is dreadful."

Mr. Schiffner rummaged about in his pile of music.

"Play this for me," he commanded. Robert stared at the music. How strange! It was full of mistakes.

"You did not play all the notes," said Mr. Schiffner at the end.

"They are wrong on the music. I played the right notes, sir."

"Good boy!" cried Mr. Schiffner. "You are a fine musician. You can borrow my piano."

One day, a package was delivered to August Schumann's bookstore by mistake. It contained all the orchestral parts for an overture to an opera.

"Don't send it back yet, Father," pleaded Robert. "I want to perform it."

Robert invited his friends to come to his house. One played the clarinet and two played the flute. There were two horn players and two violinists.

"We'll give a concert," they said.

Mr. Schumann's piano was very old and sounded awful. Robert's father listened to the boys rehearsing and decided to give Robert a surprise. When the young musicians arrived for their concert, they found a beautiful new piano for Robert and brand new music stands for the other players.

"Oh, thank you, Father," cried Robert. "I'll work hard and make you proud of me." And he kept his promise.

Robert Schumann became a great composer. Sadly, he damaged one of his fingers and was unable to play the piano, but he married a brilliant pianist, Clara, who played his music all over the world. They had eight children. Robert loved children and composed a set of piano pieces called Childhood Scenes, including Knight of the Hobbyhorse, A Curious Tale, An Important Event, Child Falling Asleep, and the most famous one, Dreaming.